Online Dating Is Hell

CASSIE LEIGH

CONTENTS

INTRODUCTION

Here's the deal. Online dating sucks.

It really does. At least it does for me.

I'm a judgmental, difficult, thirty-something woman who is perfectly fine being single.

Not exactly the flexible and accommodating type, you know?

But I keep trying this online dating thing, because I really would kinda, sorta like to find someone to share my life with. And since my hobbies involve solo hiking, reading, and cooking, and I work from home, online dating always seems to be the best option.

(It's not. But I can at least deceive myself into thinking that I'm actually trying to meet someone. Works for a good six months before I look myself in the eye and say, "Who are you kidding?")

I join these sites and inevitably end up wondering what the hell I was thinking.

I should *know* better by now.

There are so many douchebags out there. You know the ones—Mr. "I'll shoot you a one-line e-mail because I see you're online in the hopes that I can convince you to send me fun pictures."

Or Mr. "I just got out of a relationship and think all women are horrible people but still want some action so am going to try to get all I can out of this."

Don't get me wrong.

There are also a ton of decent men on these sites, too. And they genuinely want to find a connection.

But man do they need some help.

The rest of this book is going to be a series of rants I have about the whole thing. It's adapted from an online dating advice book I wrote for men that I doubt any will ever read.

Hmm. Could be because I titled it *Don't Be a Douchebag*…

Or maybe because one of my chief complaints about men online is that they don't listen, so why would I expect them to read a dating book that isn't about how to score with as many chicks as possible?

Anyway.

I hope if you've been there and done that like I have that you'll recognize your own experience in these pages and we can share a laugh.

If you haven't, then maybe this will help to forewarn you about what you're getting into.

And if you're a guy and you happened to stumble across this book and are trying to figure out what you should or shouldn't do when online dating, well, just don't do the things I'm bitching about and you'll be golden.

(Or go buy *Don't Be a Douchebag*, which is written for men and gets into the nitty gritty how-to on some of this. Like how to tell the difference between it's and its.)

WHAT ONLINE DATING IS LIKE FOR ME

I'm not gorgeous, but I do consider myself a reasonably attractive woman, which means when I join these sites I get a decent amount of attention.

(Not as much as some women, but more than I like in all honesty. And that's *with* a semi-hostile profile.)

I always seem to join one of these sites in a moment of weakness.

Like the night I decided I wanted to see which of the four personality types I was and set up a profile so I could take the test.

Bad idea.

It was one of those free-for-all, contact-anyone-you-want-say-anything-you-want, sites.

(Oh, and you couldn't stop new matches from coming in. That was fun.)

I filled in the profile, took the test, saw the results, and went to bed thinking nothing of it.

Not like I was going to get any messages, right? I'd only posted one crappy photo.

Ha.

I woke up the next morning to twenty-two of them.

At first, I was kind of excited.

Twenty-two messages! Wow. That's great.

I thought I might get one or two messages overnight. But, twenty-two? I'd never expected that many.

(And I've heard of women getting more than fifty the first day they join one of these sites, so really my response rate was pretty lackluster.)

I saw all of those responses and figured there was bound to be someone interesting in there.

I mean, twenty-two messages. One has to be promising, right?

Yeah, not so much.

(Keep in mind that I was pretty clear in my profile answers that I wanted a relationship and wasn't interested in a casual hookup.)

I opened the first one.

It was from a guy who explained that he was married and staying in the relationship for the kids. He complained that his wife didn't sleep with him anymore, so he'd joined the site looking for someone to sleep with on the side. He really liked my picture and I seemed nice.

He, of course, didn't have a picture on his profile because he didn't want anyone to know that he was a cheating bastard (my words, not his), but he was happy to send a picture along privately if I was interested.

Pig.

(Just what I wanted—some married man to send me a picture of his junk. Because you know he's sitting there thinking that's what makes him attractive to women. Uh, dude, women don't feel the same way about your junk as men do about boobs. Sorry.)

Anyway.

I deleted it unanswered.

I was not so desperate to find someone that I was going to agree to screw around with a married man.

I opened the next one. It said, "Hey hottie! Whatcha up to tonight?"

It was sent about a minute after I'd uploaded my photo.

Great. A man who was so eager to contact me that he couldn't even take the time to look at anything other than my photo.

Delete.

E-mail three was an obvious cut and paste about the guy. "My name is John and I am thirty-two. I like long walks and am looking for a woman to walk with me through life."

Sigh.

I spent a good half hour putting in responses to the damned questions on that site and that guy couldn't take five minutes to see something in my profile worth commenting on?

Delete.

The next seven e-mails were a variation on e-mails two and three.

Delete. Delete. Delete…

(By that point I was drinking even though it was only nine in the morning. I was also fondly reminiscing about that creepy frat guy who cornered me at that party in college and wondering if I could track him down through the alum site. He hadn't really been that bad, had he?)

E-mail eleven was another with no profile picture. This one from a guy asking if I was into younger men.

Delete.

E-mail twelve was from a man about twenty years older than me who said he was looking for someone to have great sex with. His profile picture showed him with a deep tan and a very large boat.

He seemed to think this made him unique or special because he was being upfront about what he was looking for.

Ha! Right. 'Cause no other guy on that site was looking for sex. They just wanted us to hold hands and stare dreamily into each other's eyes.

(Uh. This is the real world, not *Twilight*.)

Delete.

E-mail thirteen was a long e-mail from a man explaining how much he liked to please women and how he was looking for someone to take a firm hand with him.

Ew.

I took a quick look back through my profile. Where exactly did I indicate that I want to be someone's dom? Was it because I said I liked Jason Statham movies?

Delete.

While reading the first batch of e-mails I could see even more men checking out my profile.

(Who on earth thought it was a good idea to let women see how many men were looking at their profile? I mean, I guess some women would find that an ego boost. Me? I have flashbacks to going to clubs and having men reaching out to grab me as I try to make my way to the bathroom. Just let me pee, damn it!)

By the time I was done with e-mail fourteen, I already had five new messages—all of the "Hey sexy-what's up?" variety.

Delete. Delete. Delete...

When I was new to this, I actually tried to respond to some of those guys.

Nothing wrong with a guy who thinks you're attractive and shoots off a quick e-mail, right?

Wrong.

I learned.

Man, did I learn.

I wrote some guy back about how I'd just returned from Cambodia and was still adjusting to the time difference.

His response?

"Hey, cool. So you went to Cambodia, huh?"

Uh, yeah. That's what it says right there in the first paragraph of my profile and it's where the funky statues in the background of my profile picture came from.

(Obviously not too concerned about anything I had to say, was he?)

Of course, I should've known I was dealing with a guy like that when I saw his profile picture—facing the camera and lounging in a chair with his legs spread wide open.

Charming.

So, I used to respond and I'd get something like that.

Or I'd get the guys who never respond again because they were just looking for someone to chat with right then so they could get their virtual rocks off.

They'd moved on to the next profile a minute after messaging me and not getting a response.

Nineteen e-mails down and I already wanted to close down my account and start searching the Internet for nunneries that don't require a strong religious vocation.

But I kept slogging through, hoping for just one message with a glimmer of possibility.

Just one.

That's all it takes, right?

How hard can it be to find just one promising e-mail?

Oh, trust me. It's hard.

Especially when you have to wade through the douchebags first.

LET'S TALK DOUCHEBAGS

I have nothing against their existence. It takes all types.

I just don't want to deal with them.

Unfortunately, they seem to outnumber the decent guys by about ten to one.

And that's a lot of crapola to wade through to then have a mediocre conversation or awkward dinner date.

No, wait. Sorry.

Awkward *coffee* date.

(Because it's so bad out there, that most guys try you out with a coffee or drink first before they'll upgrade you to an actual meal.)

(Please. Like I can't pass the coffee test.)

So back to the douchebags.

How do I define douchebag?

A douchebag is the type of guy who sees women as interchangeable and only good for one of two things— satisfying his ego or fucking.

He has no interest in getting to know a woman. He doesn't care about her dreams, desires, or interests.

He's not trying to form a lasting connection. As a matter of fact, if he does convince a woman to have sex with him, he'd prefer to never see her again.

(Unless she's good in bed. In which case he might want to see her again as long as she doesn't get "clingy" by expecting dinner or trying to stay the night or some crazy shit like that.)

No. Guys like this just want to get their rocks off.

Cool. Whatever.

There are women who want that, too.

I just wish they'd find each other and leave me out of it.

Not like my profile is screaming, "Quick hookups! Casual sex! One nighters!"

Uh, no. Not at all.

Do you see me making fish lips at the camera?

No.

Am I flashing my boobs in some barely there top?

No.

Does my profile include the words, "fun", "good time", or "like to party"?

No.

And yet these idiots message me.

Ten seconds.

That's all it would take to realize I am not the droid they're looking for.

It's not hard.

Women who want to screw guys like that don't waste time on complete sentences and full answers to questions.

They just throw up some ridiculous selfie or two, the obligatory group shot with ten of their besties or a bunch of muscle-building dudes who don't wear shirts, and then they sit back and wait.

It is not rocket science.

And yet these idiots message me all the time.

Even though it's a colossal waste of effort.

Granted, it's all a numbers game. Ask enough women and one will eventually say yes.

But I wish they'd save *me* the hassle of reading and deleting their messages.

All they have to do is keep to the fun girls with the boob shots and selfies. How hard is that?

Honestly.

Of course, I'd rather deal with those guys any day of the week than deal with that other oh-so-special type of douchebag: The Married Man.

He deserves his own chapter.

THE MOST SPECIAL DOUCHEBAG
OF ALL: THE MARRIED MAN

The worst type of douchebag out there is the married man.

He could easily go on one of those sites that's designed for men like him.

You know the one. It only lists women looking for married men to screw.

But does he? No. He messages me instead.

Fuck him.

I want an actual relationship not that crap.

Screwing some dude twice a week when it's convenient to him is not what I call a relationship.

I don't give a rat's ass if he's good-looking or charming.

He's married.

And, no, I don't really care what his story is.

So what if his wife doesn't want to have sex anymore.

Maybe it's because she's running around after his three kids, doing his laundry, managing the household finances, and working her own full-time job?

Or maybe it's because he's become a passive-aggressive asshole or a distant, entitled jerk?

Who wants to have sex with a man like that?

Not his wife.

And not me.

This type of guy especially annoys me because there *are* women out there who like screwing married men.

There are women out there who like screwing any and all men.

And yet these asswipes insist on messaging me.

Why?

Because they're *special.*

They need to have a *connection* with a woman and those brainless party girls just aren't enough for them. *Pobrecitos.*

They don't want just any woman, they want a woman like me—intelligent, funny, witty. A woman who can have a scintillating conversation *and* orgasmic sex.

But that's the problem, see? I'm intelligent, funny, and witty. And looking for a *real* relationship.

I don't want to get involved with a guy like that.

(Now, that's not to say that I haven't been tempted once or twice. But it certainly wasn't by some random guy I met online. It was by someone I knew in my real life that I spent a little too much time with.)

So here are these guys.

They can't just settle for one of the women who would happily screw them.

Instead they have to bother me with their pathetic stories about how they're in it for the kids or how they owe it to their wife to stick with the marriage.

(But not to be faithful? Isn't that nice.)

I was on a mainstream site where guys could easily find women like this and they still messaged me.

The site had questions about whether a woman would be willing to be involved with a guy who was already in a committed relationship.

Did these guys look at my answer? (That was of the HELL NO variety.)

Nope.

They just looked at my frickin' profile picture and sent me their sad story.

Assholes.

(And just a thought here. If a guy really is looking for more than just sex with a woman who meets his general physical requirements, then perhaps it isn't sex that's the problem in the relationship.)

(Maybe what he's really missing is intimacy and connection and he needs to focus his efforts on fixing his shit rather than pursuing women like me online. Just a thought.)

These guys need a clue. (And therapy.)

Of course, some guys have permission from their wives or partners.

That's a slightly different story.

I still don't want to get involved with them, but I don't think they're pond scum. Just fishing off the wrong pier.

Those men need to join a polyamory group or look for women open to that kind of thing.

And they need to leave women like me who want committed monogamous one-to-one relationships out of it.

Seriously! Leave me alone!

AND THEN THERE'S YOUR AVERAGE GUY

Awful to say, but once you get past the garden variety and married brand of douchebags, you're left with a bunch of guys who generally have good intentions about dating but happen to be completely awkward or clueless about it.

(There are a few exceptions to this, but they don't stick around for long. Because they get on there, find a new girlfriend, and get back off.)

I know they're trying.

But that's kinda the worst part.

They're trying, and yet they're still getting so much of it so wrong.

A lot like the real world, I guess.

Most guys online are like that dude you share a cubicle wall with who eats smelly foods at lunchtime and never quite manages to say what he wants to say in the weekly group meeting.

You feel sorry for him, but you really wish they'd fire him so you didn't have to smell his food every day and listen to him talk and talk and talk and say nothing.

Well, that's how I feel about most of the men I see online.

I wish they'd go away.

I feel bad for them. I do.
I just don't want to have to deal with them.
So what do they do wrong? Oh, let's see…

RANT ONE:
LOOK PAST THE SMILE, PLEASE!

I'll admit it. I'm vain.

I'm not going to put up a bad photo of myself.

I'm not going to put up a fake one either. Or one from a decade ago. But I am going to put up one that shows off my positive attributes.

And one of those is my smile.

So I get a lot of comments like, "Pretty smile!"

You'd think this would be a good thing, right?

It's not.

It's actually a problem.

Because men see my photo and they immediately think that I'm a good match for them.

They imagine me sitting across the table from them, smiling and listening sympathetically while they talk about what a tough day they had at work.

They don't even stop to ask themselves whether anything in my profile matches this rosy picture they have of our future together.

Do we share interests or values?

They don't know.

They also don't care.

I have a pretty smile. Isn't that enough?

Uh, no.

Drives me nuts.

For example, I cuss in my profile.

(Kinda like I do in this book.)

And yet I'll get messages from extremely conservative men who would never consider cussing and find it offensive.

Do they imagine that I'm not going to cuss in person when I do in my profile?

I also list boring hobbies in my profile. Solo hiking, reading, TV watching.

(Yes, that is a hobby. Shut up.)

So, here I am with all these boring, mostly sedentary interests.

And who writes me? Men training for marathons.

(Is it that lots of men training for marathons are on these sites? Or do I just attract them for some reason?)

My profile also says I regularly drink beer.

Do these marathon men?

NO!

So, what are we going to do? Go on a date where I drink three beers and order bacon potato skins while he drinks water and has pasta?

That doesn't sound fun.

Sometimes it isn't the common interests that's the issue.

It's that the guy is nice and I'm not.

I'm snarky, obnoxious, and hostile. And that's me at my best.

And yet I get messages from men who are clearly sweet and accommodating.

Why??

Turning guys like that down feels about as bad as kicking a puppy.

(I've never kicked a puppy, but I have to imagine it would be a horrible feeling.)

Maybe they think that since they're nice and accommodating they can work with any woman?

Oh how wrong they are.

When I'm upset, I need space to sort my shit —not some guy hovering around offering foot massages and a sympathetic ear.

Honestly, I think all men, even the nice and accommodating ones, tend to focus too much on physical appearance at the cost of compatibility.

So the nice ones end up chasing women like me who tear them to shreds.

(The other guys get shredded, too, but they don't take it personally the way the nice ones do.)

It sucks to be the woman on the receiving end of the nice guy message.

Or the wholly incompatible message.

I can see immediately that it is not going to end well.

But I have to be the one that ends it, because the guy has no clue yet.

He's still focused on my smile.

This is what men should do:

They should *completely* ignore the woman's photo.

They should read her profile first and decide whether there's any compatibility there whatsoever.

Only then should they decide if she's attractive.

Sounds easy, right?

Compatible? Yes. Attractive? Yes. Okay, reach out.

What most men do:

Attractive? Yes. Reach out.

It kills me.

Because it puts all the effort on my shoulders.

Honestly, I feel like I spend the time up to the third date trying to rein things in because all the guy is thinking about is whether he's going to get laid.

And when that might happen.

He doesn't hear a damned word I say.

Which means I have to be the one looking for the red flags that we aren't compatible.

It sucks.

I just want to get lost in the moment and drown in his blue eyes.

But, no.

I have to make sure that he's not a raging gun advocate with a bunker in the hills.

Or a hyper-conservative man from money who expects me to spend my weekends at the club wearing tennis whites.

Or a pot-smoking slacker who lives in his thirty-year-old van. (Or with his mother.)

I wish I were less vain than I am, because then I'd just post a crap photo.

But men are men.

And I'm afraid I'd be even more bummed out by the online dating experience if I tried that.

At least now I get some decent-looking guys messaging me. (Even if they are douchebags most of the time.)

RANT TWO:
LIAR, LIAR, PANTS ON FIRE

In my last foray into online dating, I saw at least two profiles where the guys were over forty but listed their ages as thirty-nine because they didn't want to get left out of searches.

Bullshit.

Those guys were insecure.

They turned forty and it freaked them out, so they thought the best approach was to lie about it.

You know what that tells me about them? That they're liars.

And guys who lie are douchebags.

There is no "turning forty" exception.

A lie is a lie.

They probably think it's no big deal.

They admitted it in their profiles, didn't they?

So, it's all okay, right?

Wrong.

A relationship should be built upon openness and trust.

And if a guy thinks it's no big deal to lie about his age, what else will he lie about?

What happens when he loses his job?

Is he one of those guys that will pretend to still have a job, dress up in his suit every morning, and go sit at Starbucks all day rather than tell his partner that he's unemployed?

That's not what a woman wants.

It's at least not what I want.

I haven't even met this guy yet and he's already broken my trust.

I just wish men would be who they are.

Wouldn't it be nice if they listed their real hobbies? And real profession?

I once had some guy say he was a lawyer when he was just an assistant to one.

Why? What did that get him?

I had another say he drew comics in his spare time.

When I asked to see them, turns out he'd drawn one comic two years ago.

Not that I was only interested in those men for their careers or hobbies, but seriously.

Why lie about something like that?

I'm looking for a real relationship, which means I pay attention to what a guy tells me.

And the notion that a man can make a woman fall in love with him and then tell her the truth and she'll stay? That's a bunch of crap.

Lies are a shaky foundation to build a relationship on.

Of course, not every woman is going to walk away like I would.

Unfortunately, there are lots of forgiving types out there who will probably let those "little" lies slide.

Stop that! Right now.

Think about it.

Do you want to be with a man who can't be honest about who he is?

You're supposed to be the one person he can trust to know the real him. And if he can't trust you, how do you face the world together?

He doesn't have your back. Not if he's lying to you.

I guess men figure it's the only way to get "that" woman.

Maybe.

But does it ever occur to them that "that" woman isn't the right one for them if they have to lie to get her?

RANT THREE:
WAIT, WHY ARE YOU NOTHING LIKE YOUR PHOTO?

Men insist on posting photos that don't look a thing like them.

(I know. Women do it, too. But I don't have to date women.)

I understand *why* they do it.

I just disagree with it.

What good does it do me to see the one great photo of this guy taken at a wedding ten years ago?

Sure, it may be the only photo he's ever taken where he looked that good.

But that was one day ten years ago.

He doesn't look like that now.

Seriously, he needs to just let it go.

If he didn't think it was important enough to put in the effort to keep looking like that, why show me what he once was? Or could've been if he'd kept trying?

(Look. I'm not who I was back then either. But I don't pretend to be.)

If a man is serious about meeting someone, then he should show who he is *now* even if that is a mid-thirties, office-bound, computer nerd.

What I don't understand is what they think it will accomplish to use some old or fake photo.

I mean it's not like they're going to get plastic surgery before the date, right?

And not like the woman won't notice when they finally do meet.

Don't get me wrong.

I like a good-looking man.

No doubt about it.

But looks can be very subjective.

If I were to line up all of the men who have attracted me over the years, there would be a surprising amount of variety there.

And I'd say most of them are not 10's.

I want a man that's charming. And funny. And intelligent.

That's what matters.

Sure. Looks are part of the equation.

But they are what they are. And guys should own that.

Fact of the matter is, confidence will do far more for a guy than all the hot photos in the world.

RANT FOUR:
HOW COME YOU DO NOTHING YOUR PHOTOS SHOW YOU DOING?

Of course, a guy using old or touched up photos isn't the only issue.

Too often men feel this need to post photos of themselves looking like someone they aren't.

So a guy will post that one photo of that one party he went to a year ago, even though he's actually the quiet, dinner at home, type.

(I can't count the number of tuxedo photos I've seen that were from some wedding the guy attended. Complete with indications that there was a woman in the photo before he cropped it. Please, no.)

Or a guy will put up a photo of that one tandem skydive he did five years ago that he only did because his best friend threatened to publish certain photos from college if he didn't agree to it.

(As a former skydiver, a photo of a guy walking through a field after "skydiving" without a rig on screams poser to me.)

In my opinion if it's not representative of who the guy is right now and what his interests are, he shouldn't use it.

Don't get me wrong.

If a guy is adventurous and wants to post pictures that show that and some are one-offs, that's fine.

(Honestly, how many times can you go diving with sharks?)

But if he's done two adventurous things in his entire life and those are the pictures he chooses to post, he's just creating a false impression of himself that he now has to live up to.

True story: I had some guy reach out to me who it turns out was a fairly successful and interesting entrepreneur.

His profile picture (and user name) made him look like a street punk.

He had the baseball cap tilted to the side, baggy clothes, a sports jersey —the whole deal.

I think he was even throwing a "hang tough" sign.

The guy in that photo was of no interest to me.

This guy wasn't even like that anymore.

But that's what he was showing to prospective partners.

Not a good idea.

Worst, of course, are the guys who don't post a photo.

Early on I actually corresponded with a guy like this out of the naïve, optimistic view that maybe he was just so good-looking or famous or whatever that he couldn't post a photo.

Ha! No.

When he finally did post that photo, he had a deformity that was a deal-breaker for me.

All he'd succeeded in doing was wasting a couple weeks and getting his hopes up.

I sympathize with that guy.

He had a tough road ahead of him trying to find someone.

But he should've just been upfront about who he was.

It might have meant lots of rejection early on, because some women will walk away based upon the photo.

(I did.)

But that was going to happen at some point anyway.

Better to get it out of the way up front and focus on the women who don't have issues with that sort of thing.

Like I said before, this idea that a man can get a woman to fall in love with him and then reveal his "true self" is BULLSHIT.

(At least in an online dating environment with no in-person contact.)

Quite frankly, guys like that are probably better off meeting a woman in the real world instead.

It's amazing how many flaws and quirks we overlook when it comes to people we know in real life.

Online dating is the perfect opportunity to be overly picky.

And that really works against people who are in some way unconventional.

I'm sure it sucks to not be traditionally attractive.

But there really is someone for everyone.

(Just go to the grocery store some weekend and look around at all the couples.)

I just think it'd be a hell of a lot easier for a guy to find a truly good match if he was upfront with what he looks like and who he is *now*.

RANT FIVE:
LOL OUT THE ASS

I hate it when I see something like this in a profile:

"My friends say I'm a bit of a loner. Lol."

What is that shit?

I ask myself, did he really *laugh out loud* when he wrote that?

No.

No, he did not.

(I hope.)

Men use "lol" *all the frickin' time*. And *always* in ways like I cited above.

Okay. Maybe once or twice the guy uses it legitimately.

But generally? Men use it in such a way that they come off looking like nervous serial killers.

They should eliminate every single "lol" from their profiles.

Every. Single. One.

(Well, at least they should if they want to get started with a woman like me.)

I see "lol" in a profile and I think insecure, young, clueless, nervous, or lacking in social skills.

No one wants to make that impression.

Do they?

RANT SIX:
IT'S OKAY TO HAVE AN OPINION

I truly believe that a man can only find someone he's compatible with if he's honest about who he is.

But so often on these sites I see men who are desperate to find someone, anyone, and end up finding no one because they come off as having no personality.

(Or no spine.)

You know what I'm talking about.

The guy who says he likes classical music until you tell him that you love rock music.

And then he suddenly loves rock music, too.

Until you tell him you love country music even more.

At which point he sends you a picture of himself in a Tim McGraw t-shirt.

That guy.

I mean, really.

Does he think I believe him at that point?

If his profile says he has eclectic musical tastes, that's one thing.

But when he suddenly has new interests or likes based on what I say?

No. Not buying it.

One of the sites I've been on asks some crazy shit.

You know the one, right?

The one that wants to know if you cross-dress or like golden showers or would be willing to make loud animal noises during sex if your partner asked?

My answers: Uh, no…

Well, I've seen guys answer all those questions with some variation of "I'd be willing to try it."

Which is fine.

If that's true.

Except I look at everything else about these guys and there is no way they'd actually be willing to try it.

I want to tell them "*It's okay to say no.*"

Really. Not everyone wants to be peed on.

And that's okay.

Why do they do this?

Do they really think that if they say, "No, not of interest to me" that they'll somehow miss out on the woman of their dreams?

Hello.

Is the woman of their dreams really someone who likes to pee on her partners for sexual satisfaction?

And if she is, why haven't they ever done it before?

Saying no to these questions doesn't make a guy boring.

That just makes him someone who doesn't like to be peed on.

Which I actually find a positive trait.

I like a man who is his own person more than a man who agrees with everything I say.

No two people are identical, so a guy who agrees with me on everything is lying about his own wants and needs.

A man with his own opinions and interests who occasionally disagrees with me is an *equal*. A man who agrees with everything I say is a fawning sycophant with no identifiable personality of his own.

In my opinion, an unwillingness to say who he is and stick to it is one of the worst traits a man can have.

(Being a dick is probably number one. But being spineless is a close second.)

I firmly believe that it *is* possible to accommodate another person without losing who you are.

I also think that it's this willingness to please at all costs that make people think nice guys finish last.

They don't lose because they're nice. They lose because they're not their own person.

RANT SEVEN:
USE YOUR WORDS

I can't stand it when a man messages me in half-sentences full of misspelled words.

Or using words he has no business using.

I want a man who writes in complete sentences that end in periods or other appropriate punctuation.

A man who capitalizes words that should be capitalized, like "I".

A man who spells things correctly.

A man who knows the difference between there and their and to and too.

Oh. And who only uses words he actually knows how to use.

I don't think that's a lot to ask.

I realize I'm not going to spend the rest of my life e-mailing this man, but it still matters whether he can write an effective sentence.

Any guy who chooses to approach a woman through the Internet should be able to master the basics of written communication.

Or at least realize that he's communicating with the wrong woman.

How hard is it to look at my profile and realize that I'm not some young thing who lives on my phone and only communicates via text?

If that is some guy's style, great, but why on earth does he think we're going to be compatible?

Not to mention that I just don't get how a man can be in a professional field like consulting or law and not be able to write a basic sentence. It makes me doubt his career prospects.

If he's older than thirty, he should really have this shit down by now.

RANT EIGHT:
YOU DON'T KNOW ME, SO BACK OFF

I am constantly amazed by the things that men say to me on these sites.

I had some guy ask me to bear his children in the first message he sent me.

I had another suggest that we snuggle up in his basement and watch movies on a first date.

Um, hello?

I want to say, "*You are a random stranger on the Internet. I don't know you from Adam, so back the fuck off.*"

Because I *don't* know this guy.

No matter how nice his profile picture or how witty his messages to me, he's a stranger.

For all I know, he's a crazy, psycho stalker.

I realize men function differently in this respect.

They see my profile picture and immediately start thinking about creative uses for whipped cream.

I see a guy's profile picture and I'm cautiously optimistic.

I need to meet someone in person before I'm going to start fantasizing about them—sexually or otherwise.

(Unless we're talking about Jason Statham. He's an exception.)

I need to meet the guy AND walk away before any creative condiment use enters my mind.

But a lot of men rush into the intimacy thing as soon as they can.

And it just puts me off.

I don't care how many messages we've exchanged, I don't know him.

And he doesn't know me.

If I met some guy at a bar and he started talking about meeting his family, I'd slowly back away.

Same with taking vacations together.

Or what sexual positions we might try.

But guys will say these things online all the time.

What the fuck?

I'm not buying anything a guy says until I've met him in real life.

(Especially keeping in mind how many pretend to be someone they're not.)

And I'm not meeting him in real life until I'm reasonably sure he isn't going to follow me home and camp out in the tree outside my window.

RANT NINE:
WHAT MAKES YOU THINK I WANT TO
SLEEP WITH YOU?

Men presume sex and intimacy on these sites all the frickin' time.

I wish they'd back it off a bit, because the more they push for it, the more my guard goes up.

I've had a few guys that seemed promising at the start who just completely lost the plot when it got to this stage.

(Like that "let's curl up on the couch in my basement on our first date" guy. Uh, no. Let's not and say we did.)

I know there are other women out there who are more than happy to have sex with a guy within hours of meeting him in person for the first time. But that's not me.

And I like to think I'm pretty good at signaling that it's not me.

I don't post "fun" photos.

I don't engage in sexy conversations with men I don't know well.

(Not that those types of conversations aren't fun on occasion. But I don't want to deal with the real world consequences of creating that kind of expectation with a guy I don't know.)

I'm pretty conservative in my interactions with men online.

And yet, they still go there.

All the time.

I had a first date recently where the guy kept turning the conversation to sex.

It didn't matter what the topic was, he found a way.

I mentioned someone who was terminally ill and he still steered the conversation back to sex.

Seriously, dude?

It was a pain in the ass.

If he'd just dialed it back about five notches, he might have had a chance of actually having sex with me someday.

Instead he creeped me out by talking about how important it was to move fast in a relationship and pretending to read my palm just so he could stroke my hand.

(Which did *nothing* for me, thanks.)

We never went on a second date and he probably doesn't know why.

Simple. He didn't understand that he was a complete stranger to me and should approach me with just a modicum of restraint.

Just a little bit. Just a teensy, tiny bit.

That's all I ask for.

RANT TEN:
IF YOU DON'T THINK YOU'RE GOOD
ENOUGH FOR ME, WHY SHOULD I?

I have a fairly impressive resume. If I were a guy I would totally get laid all the time using my credentials.

Good job. Good education. Blah, blah, blah.

(Not really how it works for women I might add.)

So, I am "accomplished" in areas where men traditionally like to show off.

Which means that when I tell men certain things about myself, they shoot themselves in the foot because they get nervous about being with me.

And I don't want to be with some guy who doubts his ability to be with me.

I want a guy who stands his ground, ignores the fact that I may have a better job or be better educated, and instead shows me that he's my equal because he brings something else to the table.

I don't want to hear, "Wow, you're so much smarter than me."

Or, "Gee, I can't believe a woman as attractive as you would date me."

Or, a real one I received once, "Man, I sure hope you at least enjoyed that date a little bit. I sure did."

Any of those are a death sentence.

Why?

Because when I hear a guy say something like that, I realize I'm dealing with a guy who is insecure about being with me.

And usually they don't even know the half of it yet.

I don't brag on my profile about how successful, educated, and everything else I am, because men are not impressed by fancy jobs or pretty degrees.

That's not the world we live in.

(Sure, some want a woman with a college education. But do they want a woman with a college education better than theirs? No. No, they do not.)

So, I keep most of that to myself.

Which means however impressive a guy *thinks* I am, he should probably double that for everything except appearance.

('Cause, you know, I'm too vain to put up a crappy picture.)

So, when a guy shows me early on that he doubts himself, I split.

I want a guy who knows he's my equal.

And that's not about income or diplomas on the wall.

It's about what he can bring to the relationship that will make my life better for having him in it—support, loyalty, sense of humor, intelligence, and an ability to roll with the punches.

I don't want a guy to lie about who he is, but I do want a man who is confident in who he is.

I know men have doubts and fears.

So do I. (On rare occasions.)

We all think we're inadequate in some way or another.

But I don't want to see that in a guy's profile. Or his messages. Or on a first date.

Time enough for that when we're in a relationship.

Early on, a man needs to show he's confident in who he is.

(And if he isn't confident being with me, he should find a woman he can be confident with.)

RANT ELEVEN:
THE DREADED COPY AND PASTE

I hate it when I get a first message that's an obvious copy and paste job.

I can usually spot them from a mile away.

They're too carefully worded.

There's nothing in there about me.

Half the time it includes the guy's age and maybe the number of kids he has.

You know, like: "Hi, I'm John. I'm thirty-two and a sales associate. I have a four-year old son who is the light of my life. I've decided to finally take the plunge and find the woman of my dreams. My friends tell me I'm quite the catch. I hope you'll agree!"

I'm not some factory-produced Barbie doll, so why the hell do men treat me like some sort of one-size-fits-all twit?

How hard is it to look at my profile and write something relevant and *personal.*

Seriously. If a guy really wants to date me, can't he take the five or ten minutes to read what I've said and respond to it?

To actually engage in a conversation *with me.*

A man who uses copy and paste isn't looking for a specific woman who's compatible with him.

He just wants some woman, any woman.

And I am not just some woman.

Now, I know that's not entirely fair.

Some guys do this because they're nervous they'll mess up that first message.

So they run what they want to say by ten or twelve friends until they've crafted the "perfect" message.

But it's *not* perfect.

Because it's not *that guy* responding to *me*.

It's that guy polished and posed into what he thinks *all women* will like.

And when you try to write something that pleases everyone, you generally end up pleasing no one.

To me, it's like meeting a guy at a bar and having him pull out index cards with canned phrases on them.

No one would do that.

(I hope.)

So why do men do it online?

I'd rather a stilted and awkward first message any day rather than a copy and paste.

I *might* give the awkward guy a chance. I will never give the copy and paste guy a chance.

Now, sometimes a guy will get through with a not so obvious copy and paste.

(Generally a really long one.)

But it doesn't last.

Because he has to keep responding to my messages.

And he can't get his friends to read every response he writes.

At some point the "real" him surfaces.

And he loses my interest.

Because that first message wasn't really him.

Copy and paste is a losing strategy.

A DIGRESSION:
WHAT MEN DON'T UNDERSTAND

The thing most men fail to realize is that other men make this whole dating and mating thing ten times harder than it needs to be.

I'm in my thirties, so I've spent twenty plus years fending off the ridiculous shit that certain men can come up with.

It's why I generally ignore compliments from strangers.

It's not that I don't like hearing that I'm wearing a nice outfit or have nice legs.

If it stopped there, it'd be great.

But it never does.

If I respond with a "Gee, thanks!" suddenly the guy who liked my legs is offering to do disgusting and dirty things with me in the nearby alley.

Ew! Go away.

It probably took me a good five to ten years before I'd had enough of that crap and decided I was better off ignoring all compliments than dealing with the sickos.

So I was over that shit by my mid-twenties or so.

And heaven help the men who tried hitting on me in person after that. I was so jaded by all the sleazeballs at that point that I just assumed every man was one.

(Unfortunately, that was pretty sound reasoning, because there are far more creepy guys willing to approach women than genuine nice guys.)

Which means that it's not enough to just be a nice guy. A man has to constantly work to show that he is one.

It really is an uphill battle.

I pity the nice guys. I do.

But not enough to give men the benefit of the doubt when they veer into sleazeball territory. Once a guy goes there, he stays there as far as I'm concerned.

RANT TWELVE:
IF YOU DON'T KNOW IT, DON'T USE IT

I have a fairly extensive vocabulary. I don't spend my days trying to use big words, but I know them when I see them. So it drives me nuts when some guy sends me a message with big words and misuses them.

Some guys think that the only way anyone will know how smart they are is if they use SAT-style words in every sentence.

Yeah, no.

I can tell without the big words, thanks.

Plus, if some guy does know how to use them and uses too many, then he just comes off as a pompous ass who's out of touch with modern society.

'Cause, really, who talks like that?

(No one I want to spend more than five minutes with.)

Honestly, when was the last time someone used erudite in a spoken sentence?

No. Just, no.

Of course, more likely, the guy doesn't actually have the vocabulary to pull of what he's trying to do, so he uses all these big words incorrectly.

Which gives me a good laugh, but means I probably won't

be going on a date with him anytime soon.

I would far prefer a man who uses simple words correctly to a man who uses fancy words incorrectly.

It all goes back to that idea that men should be who they are. Even if that is a man whose vocabulary is 90% comprised of sporting terms.

RANT THIRTEEN:
STOP CALLING ME BEAUTIFUL

I assume that when a man contacts me online it's because he found me attractive.

(I have yet to have a guy contact me and tell me that I was kind of fugly, but he was won over by my profile.)

So, great. He finds me attractive. Good to know.

What I don't need is for him to repeatedly tell me how attractive he finds me.

I don't determine my worth through external validation.

(I have an oversized ego for that, thank you very much.)

Which means those, "you're so beautiful" or "hello, beautiful" comments just grate on my nerves.

Why?

Maybe because I've spent a large part of my life having men focus on my physical appearance and miss everything else about me.

It's not that I don't want to know that I'm attractive. It's that too often men seem to *only* notice or value my appearance.

I've got more than that going on, and I want a guy who sees the whole package.

It's like when you're at a bar. Which guy is more appealing?

The one who says, "Hey, hottie, nice legs"?

Or the one who says, "Hey, I see that you went to Duke. So did I. What year?"

All other things equal, I'm going to go for the guy who tries to make a genuine connection with me every single time.

Plus, sometimes when a man dwells on my looks I start to wonder if he's insecure about being with me.

Which then makes me wonder what he knows about himself that I don't know.

Which then makes me look for his flaws.

I think, "What is he hiding? Something must be wrong with him. Best get out now."

This is how I view it: Does a guy compliment his friends all the time?

No.

They're his friends. His *equals*.

Well, then why is he complimenting me all the time?

If we're on the same level, he doesn't need to constantly say nice things just to keep me around.

His company will be enough for that.

I want a guy who acts like a normal human being around me.

I know. This sounds kind of ungrateful and bitchy.

And I'm not going to be upset with a guy who tells me I look nice when we meet for the first time.

(That's almost expected.)

But I am going to be concerned about the guy who doesn't stop talking about it.

Especially if that's the *only* thing about me that he ever comments on.

What's a guy like that going to do if I gain a few pounds?

Or have a health issue that affects my looks?

Or, heaven forbid, get old?

Looks fade.

Some people age well, but no one ages *that* well.

Being with a guy who overvalues appearance is not going to lead to long-term happiness.

Either the guy is insecure, which isn't going to work. Or he's shallow, which isn't going to work.

Or he doesn't remember my name and calls everyone Beautiful, which also isn't going to work.

Whichever one it is, I'll pass, thanks.

RANT FOURTEEN:
GIVE ME A LITTLE SPACE WOULD YA?

This is what my last experience with online dating was like:

I'd log onto the site to check my messages, and, as soon as I was on there, I'd see these little notifications piling up in the corner.

"Rocketboy 123 is checking you out right now!"

"Joe1972 is checking you out right now!"

They'd stack up on top of one another like these guys had been sitting on the site just waiting for a real flesh and blood woman to log on.

About a minute later I'd start receiving messages.

You know the type.

"Hey hawtie. Whatz up?"

Ugh.

I actually tried logging on at different times of day thinking that maybe it was a late night thing.

No. It wasn't.

Happened at eight in the morning, two in the afternoon, ten at night.

Did I take any of those men seriously?

No. No, I did not.

A man who sees I'm online, checks out my photo, and shoots off a quick, impersonal message is of no use to me.

He could be the greatest guy on the planet and I wouldn't respond.

He could be the best-looking man I've ever seen and I wouldn't respond.

Those guys go in the douchebag category immediately.

Why?

Because, in general, it's a waste of my time.

The chances some guy who messaged me that fast looked at anything other than my photo are slim and none.

And I have a few things in my profile that are deal breakers for me.

Drugs. Smoking.

Inevitably, one of these guys will message me and I'll go look at his profile and there'll be a photo of him smoking or some comment about drugs.

Uh, hello?

I don't know why any man other than one looking for a little chat sex would send off one of those immediate, one-liner messages.

It's not like I won't be there tomorrow.

A guy's not going to lose his one chance at me if he doesn't pounce immediately.

And yet men do that all the fucking time.

It's like that ratty little dog that dry humps everyone's leg.

You just want to say, "Down, boy."

SO, WHAT WOULD WORK FOR ME? WHAT MESSAGE DO I WANT TO RECEIVE?

What I want to see in a first message are just a few basic things.

I want to know that the guy looked at my profile.

I want him to mention something we have in common or something that intrigued him about me.

I want him to do so in a way that shows me he's an intelligent man who pays attention to detail.

(By, I don't know, spelling things correctly and keeping his their and they're straight.)

I want him to give me a reason to respond.

I don't want some message that just tells me how fabulous he is.

And I want him to ask me something about myself.

Pretty simple, right?

"Hey, I'm Bill. Saw in your profile that you like to do underwater basket weaving in your spare time. That's so cool. How'd you get into it?"

See, not hard.

But all too often I get, "Cool profile. Awesome that you like underwater basket weaving."

Thanks?

I read that message and think, well, he must not be interested.

He just thought it was cool I do underwater basket weaving.

Next.

Now, some will say that the guy messaged me so of course he's interested.

Except…

I have a lifetime of experience that tells me that if a man is actually interested in me, he'll act like he is.

If a man is just nice to me, but doesn't give any sign of further interest it's because HE IS NOT INTERESTED.

How do I know this?

Because I've been there, done that a few times with the friendly guy. He's awesome—makes jokes, smiles at you, wants to hang out.

But that's it.

He never wants more.

You tell yourself he's shy or doesn't want to risk the friendship or…

Bullshit.

Push the issue and he'll awkwardly explain that he thinks you're really nice, but, uh, he, uh, you know, isn't into you that way.

A guy who doesn't show interest by trying to know more about me doesn't get my interest.

RANT FIFTEEN:
THE OVEREAGER PUPPY

You know how a puppy will see someone approaching and at first it might play it cool, wagging its tail and sitting there watching them?

But when they get anywhere within reach, the puppy can no longer contain itself and starts straining at the leash and trying to jump up on the person and lick their face and bite them all at the same time?

Well, guys can sometimes be like that.

They play it all cool in the first message. And sometimes even the second message.

But then they go all eager puppy.

They message back the minute you message them.

Every time.

Or they call and text repeatedly.

(I once met a guy at a bar. I specifically told him not to call me the next day until after noon because I wanted to sleep in. What did he do? Call at 8 am, 8:30 am, and 9 am. Probably would've kept going if I hadn't finally answered the damned phone. Overeager puppy.)

I've seen it happen with guys who seem pretty confident at first, but then they relax a little and suddenly start gushing about how beautiful I am and how amazed they are that *I* wrote *them* back.

(I'm not that gorgeous. What do they do with *really* beautiful women?)

I don't want some guy to tell me that he can't believe I responded to his message.

Or that I made his day by responding.

It makes me wonder why I did.

Because I want to meet an equal. And a man who gets all eager puppy on me is not an equal.

He might be on paper, but he isn't in his own head.

He's lacking the confidence he needs to be with me.

And, no, I don't find that endearing. I want a grown man, thanks.

RANT SIXTEEN:
THE DREADED PHONE APP ADDICT

Every man who wants to find a real relationship on an online dating site should delete the phone app for the site immediately.

Yeah, sure, it's convenient.

But that's the problem.

It's the perfect way to smother a woman who shows interest.

A guy is standing in line at the supermarket and decides to check his account.

He sees that the woman he likes messaged him back, so he shoots off a quick reply.

No big deal, right?

Problem is, she had *just* responded to him.

So now he's *that* guy. The one who responds immediately all the time.

He looks needy and desperate when in fact he was just a little bored.

Not good.

I had a guy do this to me.

It didn't matter what time of day it was, he replied within five minutes.

I started to wonder if he had a job.

And, if he did, whether he was any good at it.

It's one of those bizarre situations, because when you really like a guy, he can't message you enough.

But, for most men most of the time, it's a losing strategy.

Early on a guy needs to limit his responses to once a day.

I don't want some guy to wait *two weeks* to message me back, but I also don't want him to jump all over me every time I respond.

The easiest way to fix it? Delete the damned phone app.

RANT SEVENTEEN:
PLEASE LISTEN TO ME

This seems so simple, but it isn't.

Men need to listen to the woman they're communicating with.

I do not try to hide things when I'm communicating with a man.

I'll give him signals that I'm uncomfortable.

I'll let him know if I'm interested.

I'll tell him what I want or don't want.

Verbal or non-verbal, it's all there.

But so many men treat women as interchangeable.

We are not one size fits all.

I don't value money or prestige, so when a guy tries to impress me with how much he earns or the fancy toys he owns, it doesn't work.

And he'd know it if he just listened to me.

I'm pretty explicit in my profile about what I do value.

A smart man would read that profile and find a way to tell me how he provides what *I'm* looking for.

Not what GQ or Maxim says a woman wants. What *I* want.

I'm not a presents kind of girl. It makes me feel very awkward to receive anything other than food and drinks from a man.

I'd rather a guy buy me a ten cent ring that ties into some private joke of ours than have a guy buy me some hundred dollar pair of earrings that aren't my style.

Other women are the exact opposite. They have certain standards that a man must meet—a dozen long-stemmed roses on the first month anniversary or a fancy dinner for the first date. Whatever.

It differs for every single woman.

But men assume most women want the fancy gifts. (Thanks, Hallmark.)

So I find myself in the awkward position of having to try to thank them for the kind gesture while at the same time discouraging them from ever doing it again.

(It is not an easy thing to be both grateful and discouraging at the same time.)

I'll give you an example.

I was on a site that let you send virtual gifts to people.

I found them cheesy and stupid, so no need for anyone to waste their virtual roses on me.

But this one guy would send me a virtual gift with *every single message*.

Each time, I would respond with something like, "Thank you for the roses, but really, that's not necessary. I'm not much of a gift person."

And he'd keep right on sending them.

Why?

I finally told him to stop and he still did it, so I quit responding to him.

He wasn't listening to me.

And if he couldn't listen at the beginning of the relationship, he certainly wasn't going to listen later on.

RANT EIGHTEEN:
EX TALK

I know that the men I date have a past. They've been married before or in committed relationships or they spent their twenties playing the field or in a monastery.

I know this. But I don't need to know much more than that.

Oh, I'm curious about it all right. And I'll ask the questions.

But they don't need to answer.

So many men sabotage themselves by talking about their prior relationships. They'd be far better off just focusing on the moment.

I remember asking one guy about splitting custody with his ex.

(Because, you know, how the custody arrangement with the ex works matters to me if I'm going to date a guy with kids.)

Well, he came back with some lengthy rant about how immature his ex was and how he wondered why he'd ever bothered to marry her in the first place.

It was nasty.

And, sure, he wasn't saying those nasty things about me. He didn't have to be.

How he talked about his ex told me some very important information about him and how he felt about women who didn't agree with him.

The guy who rips on his ex is almost as bad as the guy who talks lovingly about her.

I dated another guy who still had a picture of his ex on his fridge.

He made a point of showing me the picture and talking about how beautiful she was.

Not exactly a guy who was ready to move forward with his life, was he?

The best advice for men is to never talk about their prior relationships. At least not in any sort of detail.

I will call it quits with a guy the minute he starts using negative words about an ex.

You know the ones.

Bitch. Whore.

He thinks he's talking about his ex.

He's not.

He's telling me that when women in his life disappoint him they move from "beautiful" to "bitch."

And that there's a line somewhere that I could cross that will turn him from sweet and affectionate to vile and hateful.

I don't want to be with someone like that.

There are men out there who *never* call women names like that.

Ever.

Not in the heat of anger. Not when the woman has done terrible things to them.

They *never* do it.

Those are the men I want to date.

Because what a man says about other women matters.

Even when he's saying it to be flattering.

I once had a guy say something to me along the lines of "I really like how you're not uptight like most women."

He thought it was a compliment.

I thought he was an ass.

Do you think I cared that I was the exception to this man's one-dimensional view of women?

No. No, I did not.

What I heard was a man who didn't like women.

And I wasn't going to stick around to see how long it took for him to move me from "special" to "just like all them other bitches."

Next.

RANT NINETEEN:
DO YOU REALIZE WHAT YOU JUST TOLD ME?

Men really should avoid talking about why their prior relationships ended, too. They think they're talking about *that* relationship, but they don't realize that they're also talking about *this* relationship.

I had some guy tell me about how he'd split from his last girlfriend because she wanted him to settle down and have kids. After five years he just wasn't sure he was ready.

What was I supposed to think?

Well, if I wanted to get married and have kids anytime soon, this guy was not the guy for it.

And, even worse, he might do the same thing to me and tell me what I want to hear for five years until I finally realize that it is never going to happen.

And there'd I'd be, five years older, still single, and no closer to marriage and kids.

Now, it's possible that the issues he had with marrying his ex have nothing to do with me.

Maybe he thought she'd make a terrible mother.

Maybe he's lost a parent since then and it changed his perspective.

But that wasn't what he told me.

What he told me with that story was that he was the type to stay in a relationship with a woman knowing what she wanted even when he knew he didn't want the same thing.

And that he'd do so for an extended period of time.

Of course, I had the opposite happen, too.

This guy spent most of our date talking about how he just wanted something casual, and then flipped out when I told him I could only see our relationship being casual.

He hadn't meant that about me. It was all those other women he'd been talking about.

Men need to stay on message.

I don't think they can avoid saying anything at all about their prior relationships.

(I certainly wouldn't let them get away with it.)

But what they can do is talk about the prior relationship in such a way that they focus on what they want now.

RANT TWENTY:
THE MAN WHO ISN'T READY

A lot of men are kind of broken and hurt after the end of a relationship.

They're bitter.

They don't know what went wrong.

They're full of anger and sadness.

They have no fucking clue how to fix the issues that led to the demise of their last relationship.

Now, do they realize this and take the time to get their heads on straight?

No.

They jump right in there and fuck things up even more.

Because they are full to the brim of negative shit, and they bring that crap into the next relationship.

Which leads to a series of unsatisfying encounters where they wonder what's wrong with *all* women and they mess with those women's heads until the women wonder what's wrong with *all* men.

It just spirals.

It's not good and it needs to end.

Men like that need to get help before they jump back into the dating pool.

They need to let time work its magic.

They're men, though, right?

So they still want sex?

(Although, that's a broad overgeneralization and I can think of at least a handful of men I know who didn't go seeking sex after a break-up.)

Well, it's the modern age.

And sex for the sake of sex is not that hard to find if that's all you want.

Instead, these men try to connect with the quality women.

But because they're in that hurt and bitter stage, they're just going to mess things up with those women.

They're not ready. They need to wait.

They need to find a chick with a fish-lip selfie who likes to have fun and have some fun.

Then they can come back and find a real relationship.

RANT TWENTY-ONE:
THE MAN WHO HATES WOMEN

There are men out there who says things like, "all women are stupid bitches" or use that c word to refer to women on a regular basis.

Those men need to stop dating right now.

They need to sort their shit when it comes to women.

Because, turns out, men like that actually hate women.

And until they can get past that and start to see women as individuals, they are never going to have a satisfying relationship.

How can a man love and care for someone he doesn't see as his equal?

No man is going to open up enough to be in a real relationship if he thinks all women are just after his money.

Or that they're all manipulative.

Or whores.

Or whatever other ridiculous crap certain men spew about women as a blanket group.

And a man who can't engage in a relationship the way he should is only going to end up in relationships that reaffirm his negative views.

Because turns out that if a man treats a woman like crap it isn't a positive experience for either one of them.

So those guys need to sort their shit before going on another date.

This finding love thing is hard enough without people spewing hatred and hurt into the mix.

RANT TWENTY-TWO:
WHY CAN'T *YOU* SEE THAT THIS IS NOT GOING TO WORK

It amazes me the number of men who approach me when we are so clearly incompatible.

They tell me what they want in life or in a woman and I think, "So, why are you talking to me? I'm not any of that."

(It's amazing how much a smile or nice hair blinds a man.)

I'm not always a nice person.

I don't actively try to harm people and I don't take pleasure in hurting someone's feelings, but I can be downright difficult to deal with.

Yet I get approached by these nice, kind of shy, kind of quiet types.

They can barely form the words to ask me on a date.

And yet they want to be with *me*?

It doesn't make sense.

I'm not saying that these guys can't get an attractive woman. Or a witty one. Or even a smart one.

I'm just saying that *I'm* not what they should be looking for.

My profile is not an act. It's who I am.

When I get approached by these guys, I just shake my head.

Of course, there's the opposite extreme—the asshole.

The guy who doesn't care how snarky my profile is because, "He doesn't take shit from any woman."

He's the guy who will tell me to get over myself when I'm angry and leave the room when I cry.

That guy is a terrible match for me.

(He's actually a terrible match for any woman, but it's even worse with a woman like me.)

Some women will quietly accept a man like that's casual disregard.

Me? I go incandescent when I have to deal with a guy like that.

And then he'll match my anger.

And…

Ugh.

Who wants to live their life that way?

I wish more men would really think about what type of woman would make them happy.

They should look at a profile and ask, will this woman improve my life?

If yes, then they should contact her.

If no, then they shouldn't.

And, no, they should not base that decision on the photo.

Unfortunately, the wrong parts of a man's mind are working when he's looking at a woman's photo.

Sad, but true.

POSTSCRIPT:
THIS THING CALLED THE REAL WORLD

Online dating isn't for everyone. There's this thing called the real world where people can go and do the things they love and find other people who love to do those same things and form a connection with them.

It's crazy.

One of those people they form a connection with might even be worth dating. Or might know someone worth dating.

Happens all the time.

(And should probably happen more.)

Online dating is an easy out.

You can hide behind a keyboard and pretend that you're making progress towards meeting someone when you're not.

It does work for some people. It really does.

But for others it can be a terrible choice.

For those that have tried it and aren't finding what they're looking for, they really need to step away from the computer.

If that's you, pursue your passions, whatever those may be.

Although, I will say that it probably helps to have passions that involve others. Like kickball instead of reading books alone at home.

If you do like to read books alone at home at least join a book group or some online forum where people talk about books. Something that puts you in contact with others.

(Either that or you can join me in the non-religious nunnery I'm going to start now that I've given up on online dating *and* meeting men in person.)

A FINAL THOUGHT

Sometimes you can do everything right, meet a good person, and it still doesn't work. Happens all the time.

No one can tell you the "ultimate secret" to happiness and lasting love.

Because it's different for every person.

And it changes over time.

All you can do is keep trying.

Find someone you like, continue the relationship for as long as they're improving your life and you're improving theirs, and then move on.

Pay attention to what that person is telling you and decide whether that's who you want to be with.

Do this and you have a pretty good chance of finding something good for a while.

It might not last forever.

But then again it might.

Only way to know is to keep trying.

(No matter how mind-numbingly awful and painful the whole experience is at times.)

Look at it this way: If nothing else, you'll have a few good stories to tell the girls over drinks, right?

Right.

ABOUT THE AUTHOR

Cassie Leigh is a bit like the jaded older sister you never had. She's been there done that and isn't afraid to tell you the straight up truth of how ugly online dating can be for women.

If you've never tried online dating before, maybe skip this book and enter it with an open mind. But if you have, then read this book and know that someone shares your pain.

www.ingramcontent.com/pod-product-compliance
Lightning Source LLC
Chambersburg PA
CBHW071245020426
42333CB00015B/1641